Ain't No Hurt Like a Church Hurt But God Can Heal the Wounds

Evangelist Dr. Diane Hart

Edited by

Evelyn Woodward-Johnson

iUniverse, Inc.
Bloomington

iUniverse books may be ordered through booksellers or by contacting:

iUniverse
1663 Liberty Drive
Bloomington, IN 47403
www.iuniverse.com
1-800-Authors (1-800-288-4677)

ISBN: 978-1-4502-8146-1 (sc)
ISBN: 978-1-4502-8147-8 (ebook)

Printed in the United States of America

iUniverse rev. date: 12/13/2010

CONTENTS

PREFACE

The purpose of this book is, in no way, to discredit the church or to bring mockery upon the people of God. There is enough of that being done in the world today. The aim of this book is to make Christians (all of us) aware of our actions. Sometimes hurtful things are being done unintentionally. However, at other times, they are being done with full knowledge and forethought, all in the name of the Lord. Regardless of the reason, people are being hurt in the church.

These hurts can last a lifetime. If you're not careful, they can almost take you to your grave. Many saints have gone on to be with the Lord, leaving here still hurting because of people who they've trusted and with whom they've taken sweet counsel. These same people whom they have valued as friends, leaders and loved ones have hurt them unbearably.

Where does the hurt come from? The saints in the church! Is the pain real? Oh yes, it's real!

Some of the pain and rejection that we go through is not dealing with our salvation or our walk with the Lord, but many times it is caused by the opinions or fleshly interpretations of others. Sometimes because they themselves are hurting, they lash out at others.

Once you have experienced a church hurt, it should not be your desire for anyone else to experience it, not even your enemy. This is a deep hurt. It doesn't go away easily. If you were hurt by your enemy, it would probably be easier to shake that hurt off because you expected that from them, but a church hurt is one that cannot be shaken as easily.

Please note that even though you have been hurt, there is healing for the hurt, and you can get over it. The Lord lets us know that we can cast all of our burdens and all of our cares on Him for He cares for us. Why does it hurt so badly? It is because you have allowed your sister or brother in the Lord to get close to your heart. They have been allowed to invade your space. You are vulnerable and easy to be hurt. These individuals are the very ones who are supposed to have your back, but sometimes they are the one who are sticking the knife in your back! They will attack you from not only the back, but sometimes right in your face with a grin.

Many times, my husband and I would ask God with tears streaming from our eyes and running down from our cheeks, "Why?" Why were we being treated that way? Why were we being treated that way by the saints of God in the church? What did we do to deserve such treatment? Our only reply from the Lord was that He didn't want us to treat other people the same way we had been treated. You know the adage, "Do unto others...." Well, He told us to learn from others and not to be caught acting in the same manner.

I sincerely pray that after reading this book, it will open your eyes and that it will help to enlighten all of us to things we should or should not do to our sisters and brothers in Christ. These are real events that occurred to real people who experienced real hurt.

If you have been hurt in the church, hopefully you will find comfort and a cure for the pain and hurt you are going through...or are surely bound to go through. You see, even 1 Peter, chapter 4 tells us that we are going to go through pain:

1 Forasmuch then as Christ hath suffered for us in the flesh, arm yourselves likewise with the same mind: 12 Beloved, think it not strange concerning the fiery trial which is to try you, as though some strange thing happened unto you: 13 But rejoice, inasmuch as ye are partakers of Christ's sufferings; that, when his glory shall be revealed, ye may be glad also with exceeding joy.

Yes, true Christians can expect trials from professed friends and the saints of God. This can be very painful, but we must look unto Jesus. He will help us to bear it. Please remember that this healing will come in time and through the Word of God.

ACKNOWLEDGEMENTS

First of all, I'd like to acknowledge my Lord and savior who is my friend, keeper, confidante, and that's for real for real. I don't know what I'd have done if the Lord hadn't been on my side because the stuff that I have taken in my life, the stuff that I have seen.... If He hadn't been a keeper, somebody would surely have perished by now.

Special thanks to my husband who has stood by my side since 1976.

Special thanks to my little sister and girlfriend, Evelyn Woodward-Johnson, who has been in my life since 1991.

Special thanks to my little brother, Pastor Willie Hunt, and his wife, Joanne, for the numerous hours we've spend reminiscing about events that have happened in our lives.

To my wonderful children, grandchildren and church family, I say thank you.

And to all of those who have caused the hurt in my life, I want to thank them publicly because if they hadn't done what they did, I wouldn't be where I am today.

CHAPTER 1

Big, Fat, Black and Ugly

2 Kings 2:23–24 tells of the story of Elisha, a prophet of God, who had left Jericho (or Bethlehem) on his way to Bethel when a group of undisciplined children came out of the city and mocked him. They began to call him "old bald head." Elisha looked on them real hard and cursed them in the name of the Lord. There came forth two she bears out of the woods and tore forty and two children up. In other words, the two she bears ripped them all to pieces.

First of all, when there is a group of unsupervised children, nine times out of ten, they are going to be up to no good. Think about what has been happening in the news lately: children bullying others for no apparent reason. They have been found bullying because of clothing or other possessions or even the lack of possessions. Incidents of kids indiscriminately beating random people (for what can only be classified as "devilment") have been seen and even recorded and broadcast on international media. Many times, this type of stuff is not perpetuated by just kids with bad backgrounds; it's even students on college campuses seeking higher learning involved in serious hazing incidents.

We can look on the story of Elisha and try to justify why the children were laughing and making fun of the man of God. We might say that they were only kids doing what kids do best. This statement can be used, but does that make it right? In today's society, had this incident taken place, child protective services would probably have had a field day with Elisha. He might have been accused of mental abuse, child abuse, or mental cruelty. The SPCA would possibly have had him arrested for abusing the bears by making them overwork...or overeat. One cannot forget the ultimate societal crime for which they would have promptly incarcerated him: murder or conspiracy to commit murder. There would not have been

1

any consideration given to the spiritual matter. The bigger picture would have been ignored.

Let's take a closer look at this story. Where were the parents of the members of this mob? After all, we know about only the 42 of them who were killed; there could have been more, but I would say that 42 yelling and screaming kids certainly constitutes a mob. Why were these children allowed to leave the surroundings of their homes and go out of the city? Did the children know that if their parents found out what they were doing, they would be punished? Where were the neighbors or law enforcers? During that time, they were under the law, and the law stated in Deuteronomy 21:18–21 the following:

> *18 If a man have a stubborn and rebellious son, which will not obey the voice of his father, or the voice of his mother, and that, when they have chastened him, will not hearken unto them: 19 Then shall his father and his mother lay hold on him, and bring him out unto the elders of his city, and unto the gate of his place; 20 And they shall say unto the elders of his city, This our son is stubborn and rebellious, he will not obey our voice; he is a glutton, and a drunkard. 21 And all the men of his city shall stone him with stones, that he die: so shalt thou put evil away from among you; and all Israel shall hear, and fear.*

These kids were definitely rebellious because the law gave way for the parents to punish them. It also stated what could be done to them if they didn't adhere to the law.

Exodus 21:17 states, "And he that curseth his father, or mother, shall surely be put to death." In Mark 7:10, Jesus talks to the Pharisees and scribes about this law. He reinforces the law to them saying, "Whoso curseth father or mother, let him die the death." Of course we are not going to take it to that extreme today because we live under grace. Thank God for his unmerited grace toward us! This still does not excuse what those boys were doing.

Some parents are afraid to discipline their children today because of the laws concerning child abuse, and they allow their children to get away with everything. Many parents make remarks that children should be allowed to express themselves and that we shouldn't suppress their expressions. That's why in the classrooms you have children being disrespectful to the teachers. In the church, you have the same thing. Eventually these children grow up and are no longer kids, but disrespectful adults who think they can say anything to you and that you should accept it. They sometimes carry this same attitude over to their parents, leaders and even their bosses.

You see it all the time in the church. Some people will denigrate their leaders by going as far as saying, I put my pants or dress on just like he or she does. There is a lack of fear or reverence for the man or woman of God. Conversely, even though the saints should respect their leaders, I do believe that it should be mutual. Leaders should not disrespect the people whom God has placed under their care. Respect should go both ways.

My memory is forever seared by an incident that occurred during a morning worship service. The pastor asked two women who were nicely endowed (physically) to stand up, and he proceeded to compliment them. He raved about how well they were dressed and how nice their physiques were, and how this was what a man looked for in a woman. Of course, they were grinning and smiling, feeling really special, and after a few moments, they sat down. Why... what's bad or wrong with that, you say? Probably nothing, in and of itself, but that was only Part I of the story. Part 2 was his immediately calling on a rather heavy-set, not well-proportioned, dark-skinned woman whose garments were not quite properly fitting, hair was out of place, and undergarments were loose. Out of his mouth spewed the bone-chilling, crushing words, "Now look at that! Who would want somebody like that?" This put a bad taste in her mouth for not only leadership, but also for those who laughed. Years later, people are still talking about that verbal crucifixion.

That Sunday morning display didn't have anything to do with the preaching of the gospel. It did nothing to glorify God or get people into a posture of praise or worship. This is one reason why people don't respect preachers the way they once did. There was a time when people would not dare to smoke, drink or curse in front of them. They reverenced the preacher just that much because he was the one who pronounced blessings upon them. Now, instead of preaching blessings and how we should feel good about ourselves, they sometimes allow their flesh to take over and curse their followers. They try to compensate for their own shortcomings by lashing out at others.

That girl was cursed, if nowhere else but in her own mind, that she would never be any good for anybody. How devastating it must have been to be called out in front of a congregation of such magnitude! Who's to say what her financial situation was? Maybe she could not afford undergarments or was not taught to properly support her well-endowed figure. She must have been hurt! Somebody else must've been hurt for her. I know how hurt I was because there was a point in my life when I could not afford proper foundations to support my own female endowment.

I think back in horror as I remember the time when I once had a leader say to me from across the pulpit, "Come here with your big, fat, black, ugly self!" To him, that was a funny statement and, of course, some of the saints ignorantly laughed at it thinking nothing of it, but it devastated me. First of all, I was a grown woman with a husband. I was already battling with the fact that I was obese; I had gained almost 100 pounds during my pregnancy with my twins. My skin had also darkened somewhat because of my pregnancy and the accompanying influx of estrogen and progesterone hormones that stimulate cells in the skin to darken. Because of what the preacher had said, I developed a terrible self-image; I started to scrub my skin with all kinds of astringents and bleaching creams and applied all varieties of lotions and ointments. These extreme measures did nothing more than make my sensitive skin even worse.

Yes I was fat, yes I was black, but I didn't need for it to be pointed out from across the pulpit. Was I embarrassed? Yes. Was I horrified? Yes. Was I mad enough at him to maybe ask my Holy Ghost to go stand outside the door for just a minute while I took care of a little something? Yes. Did I retaliate or say something derogatory out of my mouth? Oh, no! I dared not. Why not, you say? Well, I did not because we were taught to respect our elders and especially the man or woman of God even if he or she were wrong. The scripture from Psalms 105:15 was constantly quoted to us: "Touch not mine anointed, and do my prophets no harm." We were told the story of Saul and David and how, although David had the prime opportunity to kill Saul because of his wrongful doings, he did not. The Lord would not allow him to put his hands on King Saul. If I had retaliated and had acted ignorantly, all the good things that I had done in life would have been forgotten, and history would have remembered me only for disrespecting the preacher. What he did to me would not even have been considered; my integrity would have been blown to bits.

I remember when I was a teenager we had this little lady at our church who would do some weird things. Not only would she do weird things, but she would say some crazy stuff out of her mouth, especially during testimony service.

For those who are not familiar with testimony service, it is the period during worship service when individuals are allowed to get up and express themselves. We were supposed to give the Lord the honor and glory for all that He had done in our lives. It was supposed to be a testimony of victory over the enemy and, though it might have started out on a low note, it should have ended at a high point encouraging somebody that they could make it through whatever they were going through too.

This particular lady would get up talking about her neighbors who had done her wrong, her clothes, her husband, her dog and cat, and whatever else came to her mind. So this particular night, she had testified for over 40 minutes, just rattling on about nothing. (It must have been about something, but after about five minutes, my little-child mind couldn't handle it, so I tuned out.) So on our way home, I made a comment to my mother concerning this woman. I blurted out that she was crazy, and before I could finish the statement, my mother backhanded me across my mouth. She did not allow me to finish the statement. Her immediate response to me was, "You don't talk about the saints of God." I have remembered that statement up to this present time. Mind you, once I became an adult, my mother and I talked about that incident, and she agreed with me that the woman was crazy, but she did not want me, as a child, saying that about an adult or the saints of God.

My mom corrected that negative behavior immediately. Suppose she had never said anything to me or said, "When we get home I'm going to tell your daddy," or joined in with me concerning the mental stability of that woman. No, she corrected it then and there. I needed to learn that important lesson. You see, some parents nowadays in the church allow the children to talk about the saints, and they will even join in with them. There was a time when, if a child were standing around adults who were talking, he or she would be told to go away because they were having a grownup conversation. Nowadays they all talk with their children about the happenings in the church and who did what to whom. And we wonder why children do not respect adults.

In Proverbs 22:6 it states, "Train up a child in the way he should go: and when he is old, he will not depart from it." This training that's spoken about above is dealing with the Godly way of training a child. There is definitely a lack of training going on: children standing on the pews, eating in church, popping chewing gum, going back and forth to the bathroom, texting, and even talking on cell phones. Oh, there is definitely a lack of proper training. As a reaction to a parent's correcting them, many times children will remind them that they've seen them doing the exact same thing. Then the parents will retort with "do as I say do and not as I do." Furthermore, parents will try to make a big deal of correcting children in public, not because it's the right thing to do, but because they have been made to look ashamed. They correct children openly, but if training were taking place at home, a lot of correcting would not be needed in public. This statement is reinforced by Deuteronomy 6:7:

And thou shalt teach them diligently unto thy children, and shalt talk of them when thou sittest in thine house, and when thou walkest by the way, and when thou liest down, and when thou risest up.

Alternatively, the parents will try to punish the child when they get home. Depending on the age and maturity level of that child, he might or might not remember why he is being corrected. My parents' solution to that was "If you embarrass me out in public, then I'm going to embarrass you!"

If any of us children were leaving home, before we set foot out the door, our parents would tell us what we'd better do or what we'd better not do. We were told not to make them ashamed and that we'd better remember our home training. Before we got out of the car, they repeated those same statements to us. If we happened to get into trouble, while we were being punished they would remind us of what they had told us. We were constantly bombarded with the rules of our home. We were told, "What's done or said in this house stays in this house." You didn't have children who were so willing to go out and tell all of their parents' business. We certainly didn't.

Colossians 3:20 states, "Children, obey your parents in all things: for this is well pleasing unto the Lord." Proverbs 23:22 admonishes us to "hearken unto thy father that begat thee, and despise not thy mother when she is old."

It is the duty of parents to train their children. They don't have to be trained to be bad because that is the nature of a child, and the Bible says that we are born in sin and shaped in iniquity. However, they do need to be trained to be good. Prime example: you can easily recognize "church" babies. They know the shout, they know how to speak in tongues, and they know how to wave their hands at the right moment. On the other hand, "unchurched" babies know the curse words, how to smoke a joint, and the latest dances.

My background includes, not only teaching in the classroom from K through 12th grade, but also owning a childcare center for seven years, and during that time I had innumerable encounters with all kinds of children. For example, one day I had a child come in and tell me that the repo man had taken her mom's car. Now we know that hard times can fall on all of us, but that child told us all of her mom's business, even down to her mom's calling on Jesus all night long and fighting with her daddy physically because he didn't do what he was supposed to do with the money. (He had wasted it.)

That would have never happened in our house. This was not the household of the "unchurched." This was a saint's house. Like I said before, we children were trained that what happened in our house, was to stay in our house.

Train them while they are young, and they won't grow up acting like children doing childish things. They won't grow up hurting other people with insensitive words. They won't grow up to publicly humiliate others. They won't grow up to be guilty of committing this kind of church hurt.

CHAPTER 2

The Lord Will Provide For Her

This comment has been used by many great and renowned men of God. These trailblazers of the gospel have left their earthly tabernacles without taking care of their spouses properly or without seeing to their futures being financially sound. Women who have labored unselfishly, entirely and tirelessly beside their husbands for 20, 30, maybe as many as 50 years, are left with only memories. While sitting at the bedside of her loved one as he takes his last breath and slips into eternity, this poor wife finds it hard to grieve. She sits in dismay not knowing what the future will hold for her because she knows that her husband did not prepare financially for his burial or for her future security. The wife is quite familiar with this passage of scripture in Ecclesiastes 3:1–2:

> *1 To every thing there is a season, and a time to every purpose under the heaven: 2 A time to be born, and a time to die; a time to plant, and a time to pluck up that which is planted;*

The one thing she finds it hard to come to grips with is that her—what she thinks is—one and only source of income is no longer able to provide the comforts of life that she has become accustomed to, especially if she doesn't work outside of the church.

At this moment, so many thoughts flood her mind, and with the harsh, cold, reality of the situation, many tears also flood her eyes. Yet, she has no time to stop and mourn because she knows she'll have to deal with—maybe sooner than she wants to—the new pastor. How will she bury her husband? She will have to deal with the shame of asking people for money to help her with something that should have been taken care of. No money has she and maybe homeless, especially if she lives in the church

8

parsonage. Where will she live? How will she be taken care of? How will she bury him? No more income from the church. No front row parking, no office, no preferential seating in the church, no adjutant greeting her at the door to take her belongings to the office. She will no longer be addressed as the First Lady. Nothing left but memories, some of which were good and some of which were not. During this time, she finds out who loved her only because she was the pastor's wife and who really loved her and still does because she is a sister in the Lord.

How could this great man of God who had managed millions of dollars, who had preached many a sermon about "getting your house in order" neglect his duties as a man, as a husband, as a preacher and as a pastor?

I'm reminded of the story in 2 Kings 4:1–7 where there was a widow whose husband had been a prophet to Elisha. He died, and when he died, he left lots of bills behind. He left his wife in a grave situation. It was so bad that the bill collectors were going to take her sons and make them work off the debt. So what's up wit' dat? She said that he'd feared the Lord, he was a Godly man, and yet he didn't have enough God in him to prepare for his debts to be paid off. Didn't he think about his wife and his children, or did he think he had time? What was he thinking?

Many assemblies have split up after the death of the pastor simply because he neglected to get his church affairs in order! (Stick around because that's another chapter.)

You've probably heard the message that the Lord will take care of your business as long as you take care of His business. This is a true saying, but the Lord expects for that wonderful man of God to be a good steward in all areas.

In his researching of the scriptures, I wonder whether he ever ran across the scripture, in Ecclesiastes 6:3:

> *If a man beget an hundred children, and live many years, so that the days of his years be many, and his soul be not filled with good, and also that he have no burial; I say, that an untimely birth is better than he.*

Or maybe he read in Proverbs 13:22 that "A good man leaveth an inheritance to his children's children."

In contrast to the previous man of God in 2 Kings, Genesis 23 presents the story of Abraham's making provisions for his burial along with that of his wife, Sarah. Even when he was offered the field for free, he refused it because he wanted to make sure that provisions were made legally and bindingly for their burial. His purchased burial site made provisions for not only him and his wife, but it also became a final resting place for his descendants.

There will be some who will read this modern-day pastor's story in disbelief. Surely, this cannot be true. A pastor leaves his wife and children without adequate funds in order for them to bury him and for them to live off of? (Some pastors have never worked a secular job; so many benefits would not be available for the wife.) This cannot be true! But take a survey, ask around. Some pastors might not discuss it with you, but ask members from other churches concerning retirement packages or burial expenses or arrangements for the spouse in case of the pastor's death. See what will be shared with you. You will be surprised by the response for not only local pastors, but Bishops as well!

Many years ago before entering the ministry, I talked to a former pastor's wife who was reminiscing about the struggles her family had gone through while her husband was alive. She spoke about coming home on several occasions only to find that the electricity was not on. She had to go into the house with her children in the dark only because the little money they did have had been used to pay the electricity bill for the church. She spoke of times when there was no food in the refrigerator or when she wore the same outfit every Sunday. Many, many sacrifices have been made all in the name of the ministry. Yet when new leadership takes over, they are not aware of the great sacrifices. Some care and some don't care.

With all of the different emotions this widow is dealing with, more are added on. If she remains in that same church, she could possibly have to deal with insecure people. Whose insecurities would she have to deal with? Well, the incoming pastor's insecurity over the congregation's continuing to go to the former First Lady for advice instead of looking only to him and his wife. It's as if it is expected of the saints to turn their allegiance and feelings off because there is a new leader at the church. For God's sake, GIVE IT TIME! Give her time to adjust! Give the people time!

I remember several years ago when I talked to a pastor's wife who had just lost her husband. She herself was on her death bed when she grabbed my hands and spoke quietly to me these words: "Whatever you do, do not allow bitterness to form in your heart because of how the saints treat you."

This woman had been a pastor's wife for more than 40 years. She had seen the development of the church, the highs and the lows. She went through the time when there was no money in the church treasury. She was there when they took money from their own bank accounts in order for the church to have the funds that it needed. (Her husband had been a successful entrepreneur before becoming a pastor.) When her husband died, she did not need the financial support of the church, but the emotional support. This was when the insecurity of the new pastor showed itself. You see, the members would have to sneak over to her house to talk to her. They were not allowed to even honor her in church. For instance, in some of our churches when a speaker addresses the audience, as a matter of decorum, he will pay honor to other leaders and dignitaries in attendance. Sometimes this deceased pastor's wife would be one of the honorees. The members were forbidden to do this any longer. They were instructed that this was not acceptable. The new First Lady was the only one to be honored. The members were openly rebuked if they did not comply with the wishes of the new pastor.

Many wives leave this world hurt because of the saints. This wife was there for the saints: those with whom she broke bread; the ones she introduced to the Lord; the many whose bills she paid when need be; and those whose children and grandchildren she helped to care for. She was there for the christenings, the games and the plays at schools, and finally, the graduations. She was always in attendance at somebody's bedside when they thought they were sick unto death or maybe feigning illness just to get somebody's attention. She was there giving comfort and encouragement. This pastor's wife, along with the pastor, nurtured these members for years only to find, after the death of the pastor, that she was left to bear her own burdens all alone. Where was her encouragement, her "I got your back" when she needed it? Who was there to walk hand-in-hand with her when she was left to travel life's highway alone with its pits and potholes after her engine died? What happened to her roadside assistance? I guess it got stuck in traffic.

What kind of example do these leaders think they are setting when they make remarks from the pulpit such as, "She will have to bury me if I die first," or "I will have to find the funds to bury her if she dies first"? Why not plan for that day? It's going to come to all of us. Ready or not, you are going to die if the rapture doesn't take place first. Why not lay away your funeral arrangements? We lay away everything else.

Alas, I cannot leave you in such a state. Rejoice! There is a hope because, as the title of this chapter says, "The Lord Will Provide For Her." Yes, He will provide. As a matter of fact, He has already provided for her. For all of you reading this, He has supplied you with hands, ears, eyes, and a mouth to provide for her or him, as the case may be. He has given eyes to seek out and ears to listen to wise counsel.

That is people like lawyers who can help you decide what to do with your worldly possessions when you are no longer here to enjoy them. Those God-given, well crafted hands will need to sign many a legal document on your way out, particularly a will so that the government will not get to decide where all of your Godly blessings go after it takes its share of the proceeds, thereby leaving your heirs in more than just the emotional pain of losing you.

He has provided you with insurance agents able to advise you about insuring yourself so that even if you don't have a lot of money now, after you're gone, your beneficiaries will perhaps be able to live in the fashion to which they have become accustomed. Just maybe your wife won't have to move into a one-bedroom apartment after having had a multistory, multi-bedroom, multi-bathroom home where you and she made all of your memories with your children together. Perhaps there will be enough insurance to pay the mortgage off so that she won't have to suffer the physical pain of wrenching her back while trying to move a box or a bed or a big armoire on the inevitable moving day because she couldn't afford to stay.

The Lord has provided financial planners specializing in retirement annuities and morticians specializing in... Well, you know what they do. That insurance agent whom you would have talked to would have given her a way to take care of all the bills for that final home-going service. You could have directed that mortician, in advance, how to set up everything that you would need to have done for your trip to glory. You could specify for the choir to gleefully and joyfully sing about how the "chariot's done swung down and let your ride 'cause you've got a home on de other side."

Yes, you're going to a better home, but what about her? What kind of home will she have when you're gone?

To illustrate my point of providing for her, I must share with you a story about a man providing for his wife, how "the Lord will provide for her" went from being just another "church saying" to being a plan of action.

A few years ago, I had a good friend, a strong healthy man who discovered during a visit to the doctor that he had a terminal illness. Now, while he believed strongly in the Lord and knew that God was able to heal him, he realized that God knew better than anyone else what His plan was for his life... or his death. Whatever the outcome, he knew that, like Romans 8:28 says, "all things work together for good to them that love God, to them who are the called according to his purpose." So if God's purpose was for him to come to his eternal home, he certainly was going to prepare for the trip.

Within the two years that the doctors had estimated his life span to be, he accomplished much in the way of providing for his wife, his family, and even his church. He talked to all the right people, including the mortician. Before he took his last trip in that long, stretch limousine, he was able to get his insurance paid, thereby enabling her to have money for an emergency fund, a guaranteed income, a retirement fund, and especially his last expenses. Yes, he picked out and paid for the casket, his burial clothes, the funeral arrangements, and—I dare suppose—even the food at the repast. During his last year, he was even able to have an addition built onto the church.

Yes, the Lord provided for her, his wife, and "her," (God's church).

CHAPTER 3

If You Feed the Sheep,
They Will Give You Their Wool

We see in the scriptures where if something is given up for the sake of Christ, it is always replaced with more. Christ will not have us to give out more than we will receive. I'm reminded of the story in John 6:9 when there were 5,000 men besides the women and children who had been with Jesus all day long and were hungry. The disciples wanted to send them away hungry, but Jesus had compassion upon them. They found a boy who had two fishes and five loaves of bread. When Jesus blessed and divided the bread and fishes, the supply multiplied enough such that they could feed the multitude and have twelve baskets of fragments left over. Jesus didn't take the food from the boy and leave him with nothing, but he multiplied the little, and it became much.

There is another story in the Bible about a woman in 1 Kings 17:9 who gave up a little and, in turn, received a lot. In this story, the Lord told Elijah to go to Zarephath and that there he would find a widow who would sustain him. Upon arriving at the gate of the city, he saw the woman and asked her to bring him bread and water, a task that was not easy in and of itself because of the drought in the land. She replied to the prophet that she had only a handful of meal in her barrel and a little oil in a cruse that she was planning to fix for her and her son to eat and then die. Elijah told her to go and do like she had said but to make a cake for him first, and then make one for her and her son. As the story goes on, she did just as the prophet instructed, and as he had prophesied, neither her barrel nor her cruse of oil went dry before the end of the drought. This saying goes right along with the scripture that tells us that "Who so ever sows sparingly will also reap sparingly, and whoever sows generously will also reap generously."

2 Cor. 9:6. There was little water or food in the land, but because of her obedience in giving of the little that she had left, she was recompensed with a great reward. In other words...

That woman was obedient to the man of God, and it paid off.

Each man should give what he has purposed or decided in his heart to give, not reluctantly or under compulsion or pressure, for God loves a cheerful giver.

In many of our churches, it takes more time to receive the offering than the praise and worship music and the preaching combined. Yes, it is important for the people of God to be encouraged to give because this is a part of worship, but when does it become a dangerous pressure game that's being played by many leaders?

I remember one time when I was in a church and the treasurer told the pastor that x amount of money was needed that day from the offering in order to pay all the bills for that week. There was nothing wrong with that statement because the saints needed to know that the church was in need. (James 4:2 does say that we have not because we ask not.) So, telling the saints that there was a need was fine, but what was not okay was when the preacher said, "Don't worry about it; I'll take care of it."

The service went on as usual. They received the tithes and offering, the pastor got up and sang a very moving song, the saints began to rejoice, and then BANG! He hit us with it; he began to sob, telling the saints that the church had a need and that the Lord was calling for us to make a sacrifice. He sang a while, prayed a while, and begged an even longer while until he had received thousands of dollars. You would have had to have had a heart encased in concrete for it not to be drenched in emotions and exploding with compassion as a response to his outpouring of tears and feigned pain. People were so moved that they were writing postdated checks, giving rent money, food money and everything else simply because their leader proclaimed, "Thus saith the Lord."

I was in another service where there was an evangelist who was running the revival for the week. He told the pastor to collect the offering as usual while getting as much as he could and that he would take care of the rest. Each night he would preach a very uplifting message, have the altar call, and then have a healing line where he instructed the saints to bring more money up if they wanted to be blessed. Of course this worked because who doesn't want to be blessed? These are schemes and gimmicks being played on the saints of God—all in the name of the Lord!

I recall going to a revival where the prophet would call you out and say that the Lord said for you to give x amount of money. Some of those poor saints were scared not to give it because they just knew that he was a true prophet of God, and if God told him to tell them that, then they had better adhere to those orders.

One afternoon my husband and I had gone to a particular restaurant for lunch, and as we were getting ready to leave, we were approached by a gentleman. Now, basically you can tell a saint, especially a true saint of God, so he just asked whether we were in the ministry. We, of course, said yes. So we engaged in conversation for a few moments exchanging pleasantries and gradually he segued to a spiritual revelation that he'd had about me. He told me that he had a word from the Lord to give me and that our meeting like that was not by accident. With caution, I said okay, and he proceeded to tell me how the Lord was getting ready to bless me because within 30 days of our conversation, I was to become a millionaire. He went on to say that God wanted him to come and minister at our church. Now, who doesn't want to hear that God is going to make them a millionaire? So I asked him, "You said 30 days, huh?" He enthusiastically replied, "Oh yes! If it doesn't happen, I am a lying prophet!"

Well, I can say, without reservation or hesitation that he told the truth there that day. Yes, he told the truth, alright! A lying prophet was what he was. Needless to say, I didn't become a millionaire in 30 days. No, that's not the conclusion of the matter. At the end of the 30 days, as a matter of fact, I gave the Lord some extra days... just in case. So at the end of my waiting period, I contacted the prophet to give him an update on my situation. When I called on the phone to tell him that I had not yet received my millions, he replied, "Woman of God, you are doing right. You have great expectations, and God is going to do it." Then he asked whether we had decided on when he could come to preach for us. We told him that the Lord had not told us to get him to come and preach at the church. Well, that was the end of that! I'm still waiting... counting.... 30, 31, 32....

Jesus warns us in the Word of God to beware of false prophets. They will tell you stuff that will tickle your ears. They are not going to tell you to stop your mess, not if their motive is money!

The pastor doesn't have to steal the sheep's wool; he doesn't have to have schemes or gimmicks to get it. The sheep will give it up! Many times the wool is taken along with the skin of the sheep. When this happens the sheep is not able to bear wool any longer. If the leader takes everything from the sheep, what will they live off of? How will they pay their bills?

How will they survive? After being both fleeced and skinned, you have the same saints going around trying to borrow money in order to pay their own bills.

If you do as the Lord says, then He will bless you in all areas. If finance is what you need, all you have to do is ask. Recall the story in Matthew 17:24–27 in which the disciples told Jesus that the taxes needed to be paid. Jesus told them to go down to the sea and catch fish and that the first one that they caught, they were to open its mouth, take out the coin, and go pay the taxes with it. Notice in the lesson that Jesus told them to catch the fish. Members are fish. They are souls. Go fishing for souls. Go and catch the fish. With the fish, God will supply what is needed.

I remember that at one of our conferences, the Lord spoke to me and said that I should ask every person for only $3 for the offering. When I got up and spoke what He had told me to ask the saints for, someone asked me, "What?? Are you sure?" This was a very unusual way of receiving the offering because normally at the conferences, they started the offerings off with $100 or $50, and then they would go down. The Lord instructed me to ask for only $3. The Lord proved Himself because in that offering, we received more than we had ever received. Because we didn't ask for a lot, people gave more. A woman come up to me after the service and told me that she knew that the Lord had told me to do what I did because her own husband normally didn't give in the offerings because of the begging. But guess what! He gave $20 in that offering.

If we, as leaders, would teach the saints the Word of God concerning giving, the principle would work. You don't have to be saved for the principles on giving to work for you. There are many corporations that believe the principles concerning giving. The Lord instructs us in Malachi 3:8–12 to give our tithes and offerings. A lot of the other things we are pressured into giving are not scriptural; they may be something that your leader is simply asking for.

One day, I was attending a funeral and the pastor's wife was making remarks concerning the deceased. She went on to speak good things concerning the lady, but she messed up when she told all of us that this lady would take her mortgage money and even her food money and give it in order that the pastor and his family could have things. She said that the deceased's house would go into foreclosure and she would go without in order to make sure that the pastor's family had theirs.

After years of self-sacrifice—and I'd say self loathing because she wouldn't even take care of her own needs—this woman became very bitter with the pastor and his wife because when she needed money to keep her house, they did not even come to her rescue.

I recall another parishioner who helped to support a church and, by default, the pastor for years with all of her money. She lived just about right next door to the church. She even helped to buy the leader a brand-spanking-new Cadillac so that he could roll around in luxury, but when she hit hard times and could no longer support herself, she was sitting in her house with no food, eating hard buns from the previous week as a daily entrée. Guess what! That Caddy didn't see fit to roll around to her house to even check on her. She ended up having to go to a nursing home. Now, you may say that she should have said something to let folks know that she needed food, but does not God speak to His leaders?

In John 21:6 and 7, Jesus plainly tells Peter to feed his sheep. Nowhere in there does He tell Peter to take the wool and the skin too! So pastors, please feed the sheep because they will give you their wool, but please, for God's sake, don't take the skin too. They can't produce any wool when the skin has been taken. If all of the skin is taken from that sheep, what kind of testimony is that to others? If a sheep is fed, he will give his wool!

CHAPTER 4

Are We All Going To the Same Heaven?

I really like that song that we hear many times at funerals about when we all get to heaven and how it will be a day of rejoicing. It's so uplifting and hope-inspiring to think about when all God's children get together in heaven and how we're going to have such a good time. Oh, what a time! Well, I wonder sometimes whether we will all be going to the same heaven, or will there be separate heavens for the members of Nondenominational, Apostolic, Church of God in Christ, Baptist, Methodist, Episcopalian, Catholic, Lutheran, and all the other different types of churches you can think of.

It's a shame when people look down upon you because you don't belong to a certain denomination. The discrimination is not because of your lifestyle, nor is it because of the way you are carrying yourself. Furthermore, it may be that you, the individual who is being looked down upon, may just be living a holier life than the one who is perched high above you doing the looking. You would think that you would be applauded because you're in a church where you receive the Word of God and are growing to be the person the Lord has called you to be. For some unforeseen reason, people think that growth and development can't take place unless it's in their particular church, organization, or denomination.

As I travel around the world visiting different churches, I listen to the complaints from individuals, and basically you have the same problem in every church regardless of the church's name or denomination. You also have the leader saying some of the same things: unless you do it like they teach, you won't make it to heaven.

I am a firm believer that there are certain guidelines and principles that we must adhere to in order to be saved. Those things can not be argued. However, some of this stuff that comes from preachers across these pulpits is merely personal opinion based upon what they have been taught throughout the years. In this age of boundless information and sources of information, ministers of the gospel can no longer get by on personal opinion and stuff that's been passed down through the years. There is no more pressing time than right now for searching the scriptures, studying to show oneself approved unto God and rightly dividing the word of truth.

Some leaders will not only tell you that you're going to hell for not doing it their way, but they will also forbid their members to fellowship with anyone who does not believe things the way they teach it. These leaders, for some unforeseen reason, are intimidated by those who question their beliefs.

I realize that there are times when the leader tries to protect his followers from negative influences. After all, no leader wants his members running from here to there, listening to junk and just eating from anyone's table because if those members aren't rooted and grounded in the Word, the smorgasbord of messages that they've ingested at others' tables can make them sick. The combination of their own pastor's teaching and the ideas of another pastor can easily become mixed up within them and make them spiritually sick. Just one service where a bunch of craziness is being taught can take a leader a year to undo. For example:

> There was an instance in which a brother had gone to another church where the pastor was teaching the "name it and claim it" principle. The brother wanted a specific car that cost about $65,000. He went to the car lot, laid his hands on the car and said, "In the name of Jesus, it's mine." Well, that was well and good, but the man didn't have a job, had bad credit and wasn't even looking for a job. The pastor had said you can have what you ask for, even if you can't afford it.

With our talking to him, it took quite some time for us to get him to realize that God needed something to work with. His reality had to include the fact that even if by some miracle he were to get the car, lo and behold, he still had to pay the taxes, the maintenance, the insurance, and the daily upkeep of the vehicle, that is, put gas in it. We tried to impress upon him that, instead of asking God for that expensive car, he should believe Him for a good-paying job so that when he got the car he could afford to pay for it and its upkeep. The other pastor had instructed the young man not to allow anyone to challenge his faith and told him that those who didn't believe with him were not of God.

As expected, the bank did not give him a loan in order to buy the car. He went around hurt and confused because he really believed that God was going to give him that car. The worst part about this story is that he eventually thought his blessings were not granted to him because there were saints who did not want him to have the car. Eventually, he left the church.

Sometimes people will leave one congregation upset and entice others to leave with them to go to another. These same folk will badmouth the ministry and cause dissension within it. So it is necessary for the pastor to warn the saints not to associate themselves with this type of company. However, there are times when pastors will forbid members to associate with family, husbands and wives because they either don't attend or have left that assembly. (Hmm...sounds a lot like a cult to me!)

I recall an incident one time when a pastor forbade the saints in his local assembly to associate with anyone who had left that assembly. The reason for which they had left really didn't matter; it just wasn't important. They were told unequivocally not to associate with them. If members were caught doing so, they were rebuked openly and labeled as disobedient. Any offices that they held could be publicly stripped from them. If they were just pew member, they would be silenced. (For those who don't know what silenced means it's when you just come to church and give your tithes and offerings and are permitted to do absolutely nothing else until the pastor lifts the silence.)

I remember resigning membership from a church after having been a member for a long time. We cared very deeply and sincerely for the members of that particular church. We had developed lasting friendships that were not broken just because we had stopped fellowshipping at that particular church. Well, one day one of the members ended up in the hospital to have surgery. My husband and I visited the individual and took flowers and fruit. We expressed our love to and for this individual and told them that if they needed anything at all, to let us know. We were taught that it is nice to be nice. As we did then, we still do today live by the scripture found in Matthew 25:35–36, 40:

> **35** *For I was an hungred, and ye gave me meat: I was thirsty, and ye gave me drink: I was a stranger, and ye took me in:* **36** *Naked, and ye clothed me: I was sick, and ye visited me: I was in prison, and ye came*

unto me. 40 And the King shall answer and say unto them, Verily I say unto you, Inasmuch as ye have done it unto one of the least of these my brethren, ye have done it unto me.

Well, this person was deeply hurt because they felt that the members of their church and their own pastor hadn't visited like they should have during the sickness. The pastor was questioned by this individual about his not having visited. He reportedly replied that the individuals who were doing all the visiting bringing flowers, fruit, and the like (my husband and I) had an ulterior motive and that it was not being done with pure intent. Hmm....

Why couldn't this pastor just take responsibility for his own actions? This individual definitely had a valid concern. The leader should merely have addressed the issue and not tried to justify his failure to meet the needs of that individual. If he couldn't visit, then someone in that congregation could have and, in fact, should have been assigned to visit this individual during their time of need in the pastor's stead. When people have given their lives, their monies, and their time in a ministry, they need to know that someone cares for them. Loving and caring for our brothers and sisters is not a denominational principle; it is a God principle.

There can be so much prejudice in the local assembly! In fact, there was so much in the church that we were a part of that we decided to leave and go to another. They taught the same basic principles except for one or two differences. At our last service there at the church, the pastor stood up and told a congregation of about two hundred folks that we were leaving and that we would not be blessed because we were leaving the ministry. Mind you, the relocation was for financial reasons; we were leaving the area to better ourselves. But obviously, this leader was only thinking of the tithing and offerings that we contributed to that local assembly.

I thank the Lord that He has the last say. The Lord didn't allow this particular pastor to die until he himself had come back to us to say how blessed we were. God allowed him to see that the move we had made had been ordained by Him. Even though we didn't need him to tell us that we were blessed nor did we need validation, it sure did feel good to see how God blessed us when we were obedient to Him. This leader, before he made that snap decision to curse us, had not consulted the Lord. This reminds me of the story in Numbers 22 in which Balaam tried to curse his people and God told him that he couldn't curse what He had blessed. God had made us certain promises, and He had fulfilled them.

Now there are times, mind you, when the leader must openly rebuke people when they do wrong things openly. For instance, there was a sister who was sincerely believing that God would send her a husband. She claimed that she was standing on the Word of God in John 14:13 in which it says "ask anything in my name, that will I do." She went around the church confessing, telling folks that God was going to give her a particular man in the church for her husband. Well, that would have been well and good, but that particular man that she was claiming was already married. You can only imagine what a mess that caused in that church. So, because she had made her proclamations openly, she had to be reprimanded openly. Yes, leaders, at times, must put folks in their place.

Do you send those folks to hell for mistakes? NO. However, there are some who will put you in hell for any mistake that is made. I have not found the perfect person in the perfect church in a perfect world. So I wonder: what heaven are we all going to?

CHAPTER 5

It Ain't Always What It Looks Like

On Sundays we attended classes called YPWW (Young People Willing Workers) and the purity class. The purity class was for girls ages 12–18. In this class we were taught to keep ourselves pure, not to indulge in sex before marriage and to wait on the Lord for our husbands. The scripture Proverbs 18:22 was drilled into us: "Whoso findeth a wife findeth a good thing, and obtaineth favour of the Lord." In YPWW class we would sing the song "Willing workers are needed, willing workers are needed, willing workers are needed in this holy way." We would replace some of those words by saying "Willing brothers are needed, willing brothers are needed, willing brothers are needed in this holy way." As we were singing this song, we would be laughing and snickering while earnestly meaning what we were singing from the depths of our hearts. Our teacher would laugh along with us because she knew the severity of this matter; if God didn't send each of us a good man, we would be single for the rest of our lives.

My father was the type of man who didn't allow me to date just anyone. He really didn't care whether the individual claimed to be saved or not; he didn't focus on that point because just like today, many profess salvation but don't possess it. My father's focal points were who the young man's parents were and whether they were still together or whether he was from a single parent home. He also wanted to know whether the young man had a job or car. The young man's plans for school were important. Had he finished school or did he plan to go further in his schooling? Of paramount importance was what the young man's goals were for life. If he stated that he had a relationship with the Lord, that was good, but my father's ultimate concern was to make sure he wasn't a boll weevil, "just looking for a home." Was he really on the inside what he claimed to be on the outside?

There were many times when I was reprimanded for individuals whom I thought I liked. I remember one time when I came home with an individual who wore a fishnet tank top. Not only did my father scold me, but he also ordered the young man to get out of his yard. He told him not to come back half naked to see his daughter. There were certain expectations my father had for someone who was interested in his only daughter. If he stated that he wanted me to be home by 11 o'clock, then the young man had better have had me home by that time or there would not have been a second time.

I remember one time going about 60 miles away from home with my boyfriend to a church service. As we were getting up to leave in ample time to get home by curfew, the pastor instructed my boyfriend to call my dad and tell him that he had said for us not to leave. Now, that would have been okay if God had told him to tell my daddy that, but God was not in the picture. You can imagine what happened when I got home. I learned a very important lesson from that incident: as a leader you just don't override parents' decisions just because of your position. That incident could have caused a breakup in my home. Sometimes in the church, authority is exerted when it should not be. Sometimes fleshly desires are presented under the guise of "the Lord said."

While attending college, I met a man who was a minister aspiring to be a pastor. As a matter of fact, he had been assigned to a church. This young man was quite active in his church. In fact, he had been to my church on numerous occasions and was well-liked by the saints of my church. He was a very cordial young man and quite gentlemanly. He would open doors for me to walk through, shut my car door, and even buy me roses for no apparent reason. He was a very neat dresser and carried himself well at all times. So even before he asked me to marry him, I thought that he was the perfect candidate to be my future husband.

He took me to meet his mom and dad, and they too were extremely cordial and nice to me. They were very excited over the prospect of my being their future daughter-in-law. I too was excited and overwhelmed, but I knew that I couldn't make that lifelong decision without consulting my pastor. You see, we were taught that your pastor was the watchman on the wall and that he was looking out for your soul. So I made an appointment to see my pastor.

During our meeting, I told him that I had been asked to be married. My pastor looked at me and, without hesitation, asked whether I had consulted the Lord concerning this move in my life. I told him, "Not really" because I felt that I had waited patiently and kept myself pure. This young man was saved, sanctified and filled with the Holy Ghost, and he was a preacher. What did I need to consult the Lord about? Surely this was straight from the Lord because this was my second engagement. My pastor quietly instructed me to pray and ask God for His perfect will to be done in my life. He went on to say that I should pray with an open mind because God would not override my will if I had already made up my mind about what I wanted. He continued to instruct me by saying that this young man was not for me and was not my husband.

Well, I was crushed, but thank God I listened to wise counseling. I went before the Lord and began to pray asking Him for His perfect will to be done in my life, not His permissive will. I asked Him to show me what I needed to see or to hear. After praying, I began to see things immediately, and when I say immediately, I mean immediately!

One day around Christmastime, my fiancé and I were over at his pastor's house putting up the Christmas tree. His phone rang. While talking to the other person on the line, I noticed that his voice began to change from a very calm one to a troubled one. He began to tell the person on the line, in an agitated way, to stop harassing him about that bill and that he had already paid it. So when he got off the phone, I asked him what that was all about, and he replied that it was his roommate bugging him about a credit card that they shared. He further stated that his roommate was jealous of our relationship and was only doing that to irritate him. I went on to inquire about his roommate only to find out that his roommate was a male. Well, that struck me kind of funny that a male would get a credit card with another male and not be related, but I didn't question it anymore.

A couple of weeks later, I had a girlfriend who was moving into an apartment off campus. She asked me whether my boyfriend and I would help her and her boyfriend to move. In the midst of moving her into her apartment, a terrible snow storm hit that area very fast. We were stranded at her apartment. This girlfriend and her boyfriend were intimate and, of course, they shared the same bedroom. That left me and my fiancé alone together. Well, we went the entire night without his touching me, kissing me or being inappropriate in any manner. That's good right? That's the way it should have been. After all, we both were saved, sanctified, and filled with the Holy Ghost. Yet in my fleshly mind I wondered what MAN would be alone with all of my wonderfulness and not even try something. That night made me say, hmmm. You know that there are some things that make you go hmmm. Well, this was one. What the "John Blazzit" was he thinking about? Where was his mind? It was definitely not on ME.

As time went on, one of the young ladies from the college came to me and asked whether I was still engaged to this young man. I responded, "Yes, of course. Why do you ask?" She replied, "Oh...oh, nothing." Not willing to let her get away with what sounded like she was hesitating about or hiding something, I said, "No! Why did you ask?" With a feeling of foreboding, she went on to slowly draw out each word with all deliberateness as she warned me, "Oh girl, you just better pray before making that commitment!" After she made that statement, I began to feel funny, REAL FUNNY inside. I started having flashbacks about previous incidents: the conversation about the credit card and his roommate's jealousy, and especially the occasion of our being snowed in and no advances being made toward me.

If you listen to the voice of the Lord, He will not leave you or steer you in the wrong direction. That's why Proverbs 3:6 tells you to acknowledge Him in all your ways, and He will direct your paths. Well, I did just that; I listened to God's voice.

Finally I told my fiancé that we needed to have a serious talk. He agreed. So he picked me up that night, and we went to a restaurant. The lights were dim, and the mood was very cozy. I had butterflies in my stomach and was nervous because I didn't want to hear what I thought to be true. I started the conversation out with how much I loved him and looked forward to being his wife and the first lady of his church, but I needed to know whether there was anything in his life that he needed to share with me before we made that commitment. I noticed that tears were forming in his eyes and began to trickle down his cheeks. He slowly leaned over, held my hands very gently and said, "Yes, there is. I'm GAY, not bisexual, but homosexual." He went on to explain to me in the same breath that, in order to be a successful pastor, he needed to have a great woman by his side.

Of course, you know I was too through. He wanted me only as a front. He had no intentions of being a true man who would love his wife as Christ loved the church. He only wanted to perpetrate a fraud. I was devastated, hurt, frustrated, betrayed, and disgusted by someone who called himself a man of the cloth. Here he was: a preacher, saved, sanctified and filled with the Holy Ghost plotting against this poor, naïve, and ripe, young virgin. Without a doubt, that night was the end of that relationship. I pawned that engagement ring, which did give me a little satisfaction.

Every so often I would wonder whether I had made too hasty a decision. Where was my faith? Maybe I could have prayed, and God would have transformed him and made him brand new. For real! God can make a beautiful, vibrant diamond out of a lump of lifeless, dirty coal.

About three years later, I saw him as I was attending a conference in Washington, DC. On his arm was this beautiful young lady whom he introduced to me as his wife. My heart dropped. I wondered whether she knew because if she didn't, she was going to be in for that same world of hurt that I had gone through, but then, maybe he had gotten himself together. Maybe God had taken that piece of near-worthless dirty black coal that was the sin in his soul, crushed it, heated it, put it under pressure and produced that valuable diamond that was a good husband. Maybe he was the husband to her that I had wanted him to be to me.

Well, guess what! About two years later, I ran into someone from the church of which he was the pastor, and I just matter-of-factly asked how he was doing. Somewhat horrified she said, "Oh no! Didn't you hear that Pastor died about a year ago?" I screamed from shock and said, "Oh no! What happened?" In a very low voice she stated that he had died of AIDS.

I shared this story because it's a prime example of how something can be one thing on the outside and another on the inside. It reminds me of the many times I've gone to the grocery store and bought, what I believed to be, ripe, plump, juicy grapes, and taken them home to find that when I bit into them, they were sour enough to put my teeth on edge. They were not what they appeared to be. My fiancé, whom I had met in the church, mind you, was not what he appeared to be.

There are so many young saved ladies out there desiring to have a husband, desiring to have a true man of God by their side; someone to share all their joys and sorrows with, someone to have a home and children with, and someone to spend the rest of their lives with. Many of these saved ladies don't wait on God. The divorce rate is at an all-time high in the church because someone is not consulting the Lord and waiting. In opposition to Proverbs 18:22, the women are not allowing the men to find them. Instead they are going out and finding their own husbands. Many are using the Internet and dating games to match them up with men that they eventually marry. Many times they are accepting just a pair of pants. They don't have a job, car, home... Some have a felony so that many times they can't get a good job. Their credit is shot, and they owe back child support. These same women will know this same information, yet they will pay thousand of dollars to walk down the church aisle in their long white gowns even after being advised by their pastor and parents to wait on the Lord. Sometimes the young bride is not told that this is not her husband and that she should give him a chance to prove himself to see whether he is going to stay out of jail or gets re-institutionalized. See if he's going to get a job and keep it, and that's before you get married!

During all marriages, there will be problems. There will be ups and downs, but there are some problems that you don't have to go through if you would only listen to sound advice.

There are some men and women who are in the church just looking for a naïve individual to prey upon. They are lazy, con artists, freeloaders, down low, and low down. With my own ears, I've heard men state that after they've sowed their wild oats and are ready to settle down, they'll go to the church to find their wife. Now there's nothing wrong with that as long as they don't have a half dozen kids by different women running around and a poor "wifey" who has to deal with the baby-momma drama. Instead of having a wonderful and glorious marriage, she'll spend most of her life praying for deliverance and seeing that it just won't come. Doors are shut. Things and rough, and they think they're done. Then after all that, they want to blame it on the devil. The devil didn't make them do that; they did it because they wanted to. They just wouldn't wait on the Lord and listen to sound advice. They only scratched the surface. They didn't dig deep enough to find the roots. They have brought on their own hurt.

CHAPTER 6

Pull It Out By the Root!

One hot summer day, I was in my yard pulling up weeds from between the flowers. I was going along just pretty routinely pulling as I went with not too much of a struggle. But then, I got to one particular weed that was determined to stay where it was. I could almost here it singing, "I shall not, I shall not be moved. Just like a tree that's planted by the water, I shall not be moved." Well, after I rebuked that initial thought, I pulled and I pulled to get it to come up, but it was so stubborn, that it just wouldn't let go. After struggling with this weed for (what seemed like) five minutes, I gave up frustrated. My next-door neighbor had been looking out the window noticing me struggling with this weed. So, she came out and said, "You know. That's a message within itself. Sometimes, we've allowed the weeds in our lives to grow so deep that when we try to uproot them, it's almost impossible because they're so deeply rooted."

Roots may be so far imbedded into the ground that they may extend across the yard. The roots become intertwined with the real grass, and when you pull, trying to uproot the weed, you end up destroying the grass. These same weeds, like the dandelion once the wind hits it, will infiltrate the beautiful grass that you've worked on all summer to maintain. If you don't destroy that weed when it first appears, it will consume the entire yard. That same weed, if you don't know it's a weed, will fool you into thinking it is grass. It's a wolf in sheep's clothing; it can eat up everything around it, have blood dripping from its teeth and yet look back at you while appearing docile and totally harmless. It has the same color. It has the same shape. It may have the same smell, but don't be fooled; that wolf is a weed. It's like when you see the guy on the corner selling a coat by a famous fashion designer. Is it leather or is it "pleather"? It may look like leather, it may feel like leather, and it might have that soothing, rich leather smell, but it's not the real thing. It's the same way with that weed. You see, that weed can be poisonous. It will destroy.

I'm reminded of the scripture in Matthew 13 that presents the parable about the wheat and the tares when the servants wanted to go out and gather them for the master. He specifically told them to allow the wheat and the tares to grow up together and for the servants not to try to separate them because they were so intertwined that in separating them, the wheat could be destroyed. That's why it's so important for leaders to be able to identify defective attributes in individuals. For instance, if a person is exhibiting anger attributes, that leader must address that root cause instead of allowing that person to continue in that way because that anger will not just remain as an anger issue; it will develop into something else. In developing into something else, who will it destroy in the meantime? Anger is only a reaction. One is not angry just for the sake of being angry. You've got to get to the root of the matter. What caused the anger?

I remember growing up. Once I brought a girlfriend home from school. She was a very close friend to me, and I enjoyed being in her company. We would talk for hours on the phone. One day, my mom pulled me to the side and said, "That young lady is not your friend." But of course, being young and dumb, I just dismissed it and said, "Momma don't know what she's talking about."

Well, as time went on, this same young lady and I, both of us church-going, saved, sanctified and going to heaven anyhow, would find ourselves constantly in the pastor's office over some "he-said, she-said" stuff. Every time I turned around, it was some mess. I found myself asking constantly, "How in the world do I allow myself to keep getting in trouble?" not knowing that this young lady actually enjoyed throwing a rock and then hiding her hands. At the conclusion of all of it, she would go out smelling like a rose, and I was the one who would be reprimanded. No wonder the definition of insanity is "doing the same thing over and over and expecting different results."

My mother warned me about this girl, and if only I had taken heed to her instructions, it would have saved me a lot of pain and embarrassment. Additionally, I would also have been saved from even more humiliation in the church, such as being publicly rebuked in front of the entire church, if our spiritual leader had recognized that there was a problem, not only with the young lady but also with me. Her problem was evil communication. My problem was being gullible and naïve and not seeing that "weed" for what it was. It looked good. It smelled good. But it wasn't good for me to be around.

It is written in Proverbs 12:1 that "Whoso loveth instruction loveth knowledge: but he that hateth reproof is brutish." If I had only followed my mom's instructions, I would have been saved from a lot of anguish. The weed would have been uprooted, and my grass would have flourished a lot better.

CHAPTER 7

It's Your Family Mess

In the local church, you can have family members who prove to be a blessing or a disruption. If in a particular church they hold elections, a large family can sway the votes.

I remember being in a church once in which elections were held once a year for the various auxiliaries. Now, similar to the way a lot of folks come out to church for only funerals and Easter, at election time, you would have family members coming out of the woodwork to vote in favor of their relative who was running for a particular office. Many of these same folks would not come during the course of the year, but they always managed to find their way through the church doors in time for the elections.

Large families can cause dissention in the church and among each other. When this happens, they have a tendency to blame the church for their problems. It is not a church problem, it's a family problem, but the church is the ultimate scapegoat. There are examples in the Bible where family members had problems with each other:

- In Genesis 4:1–8 we read the story in which Cain was insanely jealous of his brother Abel because God accepted Abel's sacrifice and not his. Cain's root problem (jealousy) led to the commission of the first recorded case of fratricide: Cain murdered Abel, his own brother. Now I'd call that a major family problem. Notwithstanding the horror of this act, Cain was given the opportunity to rectify the problem. God told him that if he didn't get it straight, that sin would lie at his door. Some aspects of this family problem have spilled over into the church.

- From chapters 25 through 27 of Genesis, we have the next major family problem that we will discuss: that of Jacob and Esau. Jacob was the younger brother of Esau. Because he was younger, he was not entitled to the benefits and inheritance that would belong to his elder sibling, Esau, upon the death of their father, Isaac. Because of his covetousness, and his mother's favoritism toward him, together they devised a plan to steal Esau's birthright. In cooperation with each other, they would deceive Isaac into blessing Jacob instead of Esau.

The deception was devised by Jacob's mother, Rebekah. She instructed him to go out and kill a deer, skin it and put its pelt on his arm to fool nearly blind Isaac into thinking that he was Esau. Rebekah, in turn, made pottage for Jacob to give to his dad to eat while he was "sealing the birthright deal." This entire incident brought on a history of problems that continued for generations.

- In fact, the very next generation (Jacob's family) also had big family problems. His sons included Joseph, his favorite, and his brothers who ultimately become the 12 tribes of Israel. Joseph was a dreamer.

The story in Genesis 29 reveals how Jacob worked for seven years for his beloved Rachel—or so he thought—but he ended up getting Leah, her older sister. He had to work another seven years for Rachel, making a total of 14 years of waiting for the love of his life. When Rachel finally bore him a child, it was his 11th. You see, Jacob was busy filling his quiver with children by his wife Leah and his concubines, but none of them were loved as deeply as was his and Rachel's son, Joseph, and as they grew older, the other children grew to despise him. Their hatred and jealousy of Joseph was fed by their father's giving him a special multicolored coat that they, in turn, used as a factor in their planning of his murder.

In looking at this story, one might say, what does this have to do with the church? Well, Joseph's lineage led to Christ. Joseph is a typology of Christ. His family had a lot to do with the church world.

Problems in the church with family members can be many and complex. It is a blessing when the family members are united, but it can be devastating when they are warring against each other. The sad part about it is that when there is trouble among them, they sometimes want to blame the church for family problems that really are just that: matters that should be handled inside the family and outside of the church.

For years and years, pastors have had to take different sides in family matters, which has not been fair for either the congregation or the pastor. When there's a divorce in the church and there are family members from both sides who are also church members, many times it causes friction among the families. Inevitably, it causes a certain amount of hurt among the members of the church family who may be forced to take sides in the conflict. The parties who are directly involved, for some odd reason, want other individuals to break ties with the ones that they're having problems with. Come to think of it, it's not so odd at that! The hurt party wants to inflict pain on the other party. What better way to do that than by causing all of their friends to abandon them?

Individuals in the church may have been friends with both persons for many years, but all of a sudden, they have to figure out whose side they're going to be on. The good church folks have to pick and choose, even agonize over whom they're going to be friends with going forward. Imagine how painful it must be to find yourself having to choose one person over the other! Then you're in a dilemma in which you choose one person and your spouse chooses the other. Maybe your pastor chose the other too. Ugh! Now your feelings are hurt because Pastor sided with the wrong person. Can't he see? How can he do this to you? Now you've got this gut wrenching decision to make over how you're going to react to this whole hornet's nest. And it's all over a nest that wasn't even in your tree in the first place! We must not let that rotting family tree fall over on ours and take it down.

What can a pastor do? Sometimes Pastor has to take out his sword and cut off the dying branches to prevent the rest of the tree from dying, cut down the tree to keep it from destroying the rest of the trees in the forest. Pastor must be a well trained surgeon carefully amputating the dead wood, and remember: God has given pastor advanced degrees in "kneeology" and "treeology."

God forbid that the leader experience problems with his or her own spouse! Come to think of it, I do know of such a situation in which the pastor's indiscretions inflicted major damage upon his church as a whole.

This particular pastor was head of a fairly large congregation. Here, I wish to propose the idea that perhaps because of the complexities and copious amounts of paperwork involved in overseeing such a great congregation, this pastor found it essential to work long hours and very closely with his secretary. He needed to work side-by-side with her, hold many closed-door meetings with her, and to lean on her more and more. Well, perhaps he leaned a little too hard one time, fell over and couldn't get up. What do I mean? This pastor had an affair with his secretary. It went on for a while, and I don't think anyone knew of it, but as the old saying goes, what's done under the cover of darkness, will come out in the light. When the covers were pulled back, the secretary popped up pregnant.

Of course, the news got out that it was the pastor's child. The poor wife was devastated. She didn't want to leave her church home and family. She had invested her life in that church. The pastor felt like all he needed to do was confess his sin, get it out in the open and go on.

You know there will always be some saints who, no matter what sin is committed, will forgive, no consequences given, no silencing, no reprimanding of the pastor. Of course not! Remember what happened with David and Bathsheba in 2 Samuel? David asked for God's forgiveness for his adulterous, murderous affair, and it was granted. But David paid a price for that sin, didn't he?

The pastor didn't want to leave and neither did the wife. Oh, it caused such a big mess in the church! The membership began to dwindle because the sheep were being starved to death; they were being undernourished on a constant diet of sermons across the pulpit about how we are poor sinners saved by grace or how we fall down, but we get up.

Yes, the whole church was in pain: the pastor, his wife and the secretary. Look at all of the people who were affected. Look at the sides that had to be taken. All because somebody couldn't keep something in their pants!!

CHAPTER 8

Don't Tell!

Confession booth; priest-parishioner. Hospital room; doctor-patient. Courtroom; lawyer-client. These sacred relationships have lasted through hundreds of years. Why do you suppose that is? Because everybody needs to have somebody they can trust who won't tell anybody their most intimate secrets once they have shared them. For those of us who have a personal relationship with the Lord and that relationship is...say...as close as that of Enoch and God, then we can just tell Jesus all of our problems. For the rest of us, we must have somebody here on earth whom we can go to, share our innermost thoughts and know that we won't hear them again through the grapevine, in the rumor mill, on the block, or across the pulpit, to say the least. We must be able to unburden ourselves and leave the weight of the world at their doorstep. If nothing else, that one aspect of the Catholic Church—absolute confessional confidentiality—is, indeed, one to be respected.

In 2006, Pope Benedict XVI, head of the entire Catholic Church, recommended weekly confession, especially for priests, and he himself began to follow this practice. In fact, this rite has been so sacred in the Catholic Church that for breaking the seal of confidentiality, in the past, priests have been excommunicated from the Church and even executed (not so recently, however).

I know of a situation in which a man had been committing adultery and, and because he wanted to get it right, he went to his pastor and told him that he and one particular sister in the church had had a brief affair. It had begun innocently enough; he was having marital problems that he had shared with her and, as she was comforting him, another problem reared its ugly head: their affair. They both were deeply sorry and, in accordance with the scripture in James 5:16 that admonishes us to confess our faults

37

one to another, he thought that he should confess his faults. Then, as the verse continues to say, he could receive prayer that he might be healed.

So he went to his pastor to confess, knowing that he was wrong. Pastor sat him down and told him that he wouldn't be allowed to perform any of his church duties for a while. Of course, the young man expected the confession to stay in the box (his office), but the pastor unadvisedly mentioned the infidelity situation to his own personal close confidante, also an official in the church.

The confidante made the unilateral decision to go to the young man's wife and tell her that her husband had cheated on her. A worse part about the whole thing was that the wife had been going to the confidante for advice about her marriage. She didn't need more problems piled on. Instead of her burdens being unloaded, they were reloaded. Then the wife was through. The family was destroyed. There was no way for reconciliation. Now not only the affair, but church business was also out in the street. Of course in the church world, at that time, we believed in confidentiality because the leader was your little god. You didn't question the leader. He could do no wrong.

This whole incident made people leery of going to the pastor to talk about their business. There was other stuff that people had told the pastor, and they wondered how it had gotten out. There was an air of suspicion. That hurt was not only internal, but it also hurt the reputation of the church world as a whole. When the news of that whole affair got out and was spread to other churches, it put a sour taste in the mouths of people concerning confessions. People from not only that church, but people from other churches as well wondered whether their pastors had also been indiscreet with their information.

To this day, the young man is still in recovery. As they say, he lost his religion. His faith in the religious system has been shattered. He had felt like the leader could do no wrong. He believed in the man of God. He was trying to get it right... but somebody else got it wrong. Then he left the church. He was hurt. His wife was hurt. His kids were hurt.

That pastor, how dare he? Nowadays there would be a lawsuit filed for breach of confidentiality, but at that time we were afraid. At that time, we weren't as litigious a society as we are today.

I know of an incident in which an individual told the pastor about a problem he was having with watching things on the television that he shouldn't be, and it was causing problems within his marriage. For instance, when he went to "get together" with his wife, he was unable to perform, and he found that he needed to have some external help. The individual assumed, because it was the leader whom he had told about his problem, that the stories of his indiscretions would not find their way outside of that room.

The next thing you know, someone came to him and told him that they had heard that he had a particular problem. That busy person never said that the pastor had said it. However, he assumed that because he had told the pastor, the pastor was the one who had told the story to somebody else. That created a very sour taste in his mouth toward the pastor because he thought that the pastor had told his business.

He carried a certain amount of mistrust and anger around in his heart toward the pastor for about a year. Then one day a crisis arose for him, and he was reluctant to come back to the pastor for his help. So when the pastor asked him about the previous incident which had driven a wedge between them, he recalled it replying, "I told you something before, and you told it."

After having done some sleuthing, the pastor was immediately able to bring the facts back to the young man's memory through recounting the times and circumstances under which he himself had told his secrets. This proved that he himself, in fact, not the pastor, had shared his private, personal problems with plenty of other people. As a matter of fact, it was before he had even met with the pastor that the information leak had occurred. Yes, that same little dirty cat that the pastor had been accused of letting out of the bag had been taken off the leash and let go way before the pastor had even had a chance to get it and stuff it into a bag. Clearly, there was no way that he could deny that he had shot his own self in the foot before going to the hospital.

Incidents like this, almost the opposite of the previous story, hurt the pastor's credibility and reputation. The pastor's feelings had been hurt because his member hadn't thought enough of him to even come back to him and try to get the whole situation straightened out. After all, even if he had done something wrong, he was still human. The hurt was further experienced by the pastor's spouse because her husband had a problem that he couldn't share with her. Thank God they were able to get it straight!

We must all be careful with sacred trusts. If we're ever the ones receiving counseling, we should make sure that we haven't already told 10 other folks about our problem and then blame the leader for something they didn't even do. Conversely, if we're doing the counseling, we must remember that we have lives in our hands at that very moment and that we must take their burdens and ours to the Lord only and leave them there.

CHAPTER 9

You Need To Stop Your Mess

Have you ever noticed some of the older saints who testify that they have never experienced a lot of the world? They say that they basically grew up in the church. They can give you the names, dates, and places of all events. They can give you all the secret webs of peoples' lives and their families. They can tell you the split-ups in the church, who caused them and why. Then those same folks always express that today's church is not like yesterday's church and that we need to go back to the way it used to be. These same folks themselves are crabby and evil, can never agree with the masses, always have a but.... Their children, who also grew up in the church with these same folks, never come back to the church, not even on family and friends day or for birthday celebrations for their own parents. I wonder why this is. These people don't even smile, but they are quick to express their love for the Lord. Yet they are so evil that even babies don't want to be around them, but they are going to heaven anyhow.

I remember this old mother in our home church who was so very mean. The pastor would preach on attitudes and about how saints should be sweet and not always complaining but in their situation, giving God thanks. Do you think that made any difference with the way this lady acted? She complained about the young ladies' clothes; either the dress was too short, too long or the color was too loud. The young men's pants were too tight, shirts were too open, or the collars should have been buttoned up all the way...even in the hot summertime. The young married couples were showing too much affection towards each other in the church. The children were too loud, running in the church and touching the communion table, which definitely was a no-no. Everybody was wrong. Everybody—but a few—was going to hell. Nothing and no one could satisfy her. Yet, she was saved, sanctified, filled and going to heaven anyhow.

41

Oh yes, I think I have anticipated what you're thinking. I do agree that something probably happened in that lady's life to make her so bitter, contrary, argumentative, indifferent and disagreeable. Yes, something probably happened, but why, after being in the church all those many years, had her attitude not been adjusted? What had hardened that mother's heart so that she could not show love? Sometimes I wonder whether folks like that have ever been saved or if they just grew up in the church and were ashamed, after all those years, to admit to the fact that they had never accepted Jesus in their life as their personal savior. Did their love for the Lord and love for the brethren wax cold? Were they once saved but somewhere along the way didn't continue on in the faith?

The scripture in Romans 12:10 states that we should "be kindly affectioned one to another with brotherly love; in honor preferring one another." Because this point was so important, Paul reemphasized it in Ephesians 4:32: "And be kind one to another, tenderhearted, forgiving one another, even as God for Christ's sake hath forgiven you."

Even if the young ladies' dresses were too short and the young men's pants too tight or the couples were showing too much affection in the church, why be rude with comments concerning these issues? Why be nasty, using the excuse "It's my duty as an older saint to get these young people straight"? Sometimes when comments are made like that, they can be very hurtful and can do more harm than good.

Oh, I can think of one young lady who used to love to come to church and sit near the front to be closer to "the fire," closer to "the action." But by the time the old church mother got finished pulling and tugging and pointing at and whispering about her "short dress," the young lady, instead of being disrespectful, would sit further and further back to the point where she was out the back door. If a person is trying to do something good and there's always somebody finding fault with it, that can be hurtful. They can feel like "What's the point?"

While that finger-pointer is pointing fingers at others, people are looking at them sideways. They may never say anything, but it sure doesn't stop them from thinking things.

I remember one time when I went into a convenience store to buy some goodies to take home after work. I was going to kick my shoes off, watch some television, eat my junk food and call it a night. Well, while standing in the checkout line, I noticed that there was this young man in front of me who was getting ready to purchase a case of beer and a carton of cigarettes. I began to talk to him, and the first thing to come out of my mouth was, "Young man, you don't need that stuff. Neither that beer nor those cigarettes are any good for you." Without hesitation, the young man looked me up and down and said, "You don't need those chips and that soda either. That's not good for you!" Well, I felt like two cents because here he was nicely built and physically fit, and there I was overweight, huffing and puffing looking like the "before" picture for a weight loss commercial. I suppose that my comments to him officially qualify for inclusion on the "pot calling the kettle black" list. You see, what he said was absolutely correct. Here I was pointing the finger at him, but I probably would die before he would from complications of being overweight. Ok. Let me also add that I qualified for membership in the "don't live in glass houses and throw stones" club too.

No wonder Romans 14:13 says, "Let us not therefore judge one another any more: but judge this rather, that no man put a stumbling block or an occasion to fall in his brother's way." Matthews 7:3 says, "why beholdest thou the mote that is in thy brother's eye, but considerest not the beam that is in thine own eye?"

If God allows us to see something in an individual, it might be meant for us to just intercede on that person's behalf. If the young man in the store was a sinner, he was probably doing what sinners do. How dare I give him something about me to point a finger back at when I was doing wrong myself? Surely I didn't need those chips or soda. I didn't need to criticize him because that would be the job of the Holy Ghost once he had received it. The Holy Ghost would convict. I should have made conversation with him, asking what church he attended, told him of God's love for him, anything but stand there and point a finger. I was straining at a gnat, but I was swallowing a camel.

That's what the older lady in my former church would do. She became the judge and the jury. She pronounced sentence on all of us who did wrong in her sight. All of us were on our way to hell!

I once knew a pastor who, during her heyday, was very strict and did not leave any room for error. She preached against sin and did not tolerate anyone who was caught in sin, regardless of who or what it was. The pastor became very ill in her latter years and had to be hospitalized. Because of her excruciating pain while in the hospital, she was put on very high dosages of strong medication. But let me tell you that this same pastor who preached hard against sin, who didn't have any mercy on anyone was heard in the hospital constantly cursing up a storm at the top of her lungs because the pain was so unbearable before she died. Was she out of her head? Was it the medication? I don't know, but because she had been so hard on others by not letting anything slide, guess what people talked about! Her cursing and her supposed "walk with the Lord."

> Many of us are guilty of taking scriptures out of context or cherry-picking or just stopping when we get to the end of the part we want to use. In order to get the full meaning of the scripture, we must read before, during, and after a particular verse in order to experience the richness of God's Word.

This pastor would have been well served in her walk with the Lord to take a few more steps down the path of the Lord's Prayer in Matthew 6, past the traditional "Amen" in verse 13, to verses 14 and 15:

14 For if ye forgive men their trespasses, your heavenly Father will also forgive you: 15 But if ye forgive not men their trespasses, neither will your Father forgive your trespasses.

I am reminded of the story in Matthew 18:21–35 in which a particular man owed his lord some money that he could not repay. The lord's punishment was for him and his entire family to be sold as payment for his debt. He asked the lord to have mercy on him, and the lord did. Similarly, this same man had a debtor who owed him money. He went out and roughhoused the man while trying to make him pay back something that he also did not have. The guy begged for the lender to give him some time to pay the bill, but he wouldn't. The debtor was thrown into jail. When the lord was told what his former debtor had done, the lord asked him why he hadn't had compassion on that individual just as he had received from him. As payment for his unforgiveness and lack of compassion, this man who originally had been forgiven of his debt had his forgiveness revoked. He was tormented until he had paid the previously forgiven debt in full.

True forgiveness, true mercy, true love comes from the heart, and the Lord knows when someone is really showing it. People have the tendency to want you to show mercy toward them when they've gotten caught up in some mess but don't want to show mercy toward you when you need it.

I am reminded of the story in John 8: 3–11 when the scribes and Pharisees brought a woman to Jesus who had been caught in the act of adultery. The religious folks brought her to Jesus, but it was not really because of what she had done; they were trying to set Jesus up and trap him. However, it didn't go like they wanted it to. He told them that he who was without sin should cast the first stone at her. Then Jesus began to write something in the dirt. The Bible doesn't say what he wrote, but I wonder whether he was writing down the names of some of those same men who were standing there accusing her. Hmm... It had to be something profound because they soon got out of his face and went the other way. They wanted him to let them stone just her, but then, it took two to tango. Didn't it? Where was the man with whom she had been committing adultery? Why didn't they bring him also to Jesus?

People in the church have got to stop their mess. They have got to stop the blame game. They must take responsibilities for their own actions. If they don't, the mess that they make might just mess them up too.

CHAPTER 10

You Ain't Dead Yet?

As young married saints, we can sometimes do some dumb things. Thank God for His mercy toward us!

There were times when we wanted to attend the church conventions just like the other couples, but usually we would not go because financially we were not able to carry all of our children with us. Well, right before one convention, we had a saint come to us and volunteer to come over to our house and watch the kids for a few days while we were gone. We just knew it would be okay because this individual was saved, sanctified, and going to heaven anyhow.

Upon returning home, the kids told us that they didn't want to stay with this person any more. We thought that they were saying this just because they wanted to go along with us. Come to find out the young lady would go into our bedroom, get on our bed and fantasize about being me and making love to my husband. How sick!! How do I know this to be true? I got it, as they say, straight from the horse's mouth; she confessed to me her desire to have my husband.

As time went on and I was dealing with the stress of this situation, I became ill. I couldn't think straight; nothing made much sense; everything seemed foggy. Not knowing what was wrong, I prayed and ask God what was wrong with me; why I was so sickly. Even the doctor couldn't diagnose what was wrong with me. The Lord sent my cousin from Georgia up for the family reunion, and she came to our house. Well, this cousin was a true prophet of God because the things that she knew, I certainly hadn't told her.

The very first thing she did was to enumerate, one-by-one, all of my ailments and how they were making me feel. She went on to ask me if I knew this particular person, and she called her by name. My husband

and I both said, "Yes." She then went on to say that this individual had "rooted" me and wanted me dead in order to have my husband. She began to give me blessed oil in water to drink and prayed for me. Whatever that adulterous woman (since she had already committed it in her heart) had caused to grow inside of me came out when I went to the bathroom. The dirty blackness of evil came out in the stool. My cousin went on to tell us that the individual was going to confess what she had done.

Unlike in the case of the "lying prophet" I mentioned earlier, those things that my cousin had said surely came to pass. A few months later, that sister sauntered up to me with all boldness and said, "You ain't dead yet?!" She added that she wished I were dead so that she could have my husband. There was the confession, and it was so.

I want you to know right here and now that God is a God of all knowledge. He knew enough to have King James sanction the book of Isaiah for inclusion in the Holy Bible. You see, God knew that poor me was going to have a serious need for the scripture found in Isaiah 26:3, and I truly thank God that it was included as follows: "Thou wilt keep him in perfect peace, whose mind is stayed on thee: because he trusteth in thee." I had to keep my mind stayed on the Lord, and I had to trust him just to keep my mind at peace. If not, I might have snapped. I was close to the edge, and I found myself having to delight myself in the law of the Lord and meditate in it both day and night. I'd sit down for a moment at dinner, and there she was. I'd try to read a book or watch a television show (with those chips and soda that I liked so well), and there she was. At night, I'd try to take a respite from the cares of the day, and there she was...right beside me, no doubt! After all, how dare she get in my bed?! Above and beyond that, how did she have the unmitigated gall to get in my face and confess to me that she wanted me dead in order to get my husband?

So, I'm guessing that during the time that her pastor taught from the 20th chapter of Exodus concerning the Ten Commandments, she was asleep, or maybe she was sitting there scheming a way to accomplish her evil deeds. You see, my Bible in Exodus 20 contains the following very important verses:

14 Thou shalt not commit adultery. 15Thou shalt not steal. 17 Thou shalt not covet thy neighbour's house, thou shalt not covet thy neighbour's wife....

Maybe because the scripture said not to covet "thy neighbour's wife," she thought it was okay to covet "thy neighbour's husband." Now right here is where I think she must have stopped listening and didn't go home to study the entire scripture or the rest of the scripture or even the rest of the verse.

> Remember that? Here we go with taking scriptures out of context or just stopping when we get to the end of the part we want to use.

If she had continued reading, she would have benefitted greatly from incorporating the rest of the verse into her life. It included the next little concluding bit of important information:

17...*nor his manservant, nor his maidservant, nor his ox, nor his ass, nor any thing that is thy neighbour's.*

Clearly, the "anything that is thy neighbour's" included my husband.

How can anyone who is a Bible-reading, Bible-taught, Bible-toting, Bible-believing Christian lose the fear of God to the point where they can blatantly lose all regard for the consequences of sin? Even the people to whom Moses was presenting the Ten Commandments knew enough to reverse course when they all experienced the thunderings, and the lightnings, and the noise of the trumpet, and the mountain smoking from which Moses had descended; they moved back and stood far away.

Was I hurt by this woman whom I thought was a friend? Oh, yes! Was I even more devastated because she was a saint in the church? Beyond a shadow of a doubt, absolutely! You expect people in the world to be smiling in your face while all the time wanting to take your place. However, you expect to be able to turn your back around in front of a saved, sanctified, Holy-Ghost-filled, fire-baptized sister in the church and still have every ounce of 10 pints of blood in your body when you turn back around.

Thank God my situation didn't end up like it did for poor Uriah the Hittite! (See 2 Samuel 11.)

CONCLUSION

Ain't no hurt like a church hurt, but God can heal the wounds.

I can imagine that a few questions have come up as you've read through each chapter. Some of these may have come to mind:

1. Why me? What did I do to deserve this?
2. Now, what do I do to get rid of my pain? How will God heal me?
3. What can I do to make sure that I don't hurt somebody else or that somebody else doesn't hurt me?

First, let's look at number 1: Why me? What did I do to deserve this?

Well, first you must know that offenses will come in our faith walk, but God will be walking along with us holding our hand. Why you, you say? Well, Jesus told us all in advance, in Matthew 5:44, that we should love our enemies, bless them that curse us, do good to them that hate us, and pray for them that despitefully use and persecute us. Note that this is not a conditional statement implying that these things might happen; it clearly is saying to me that these things WILL happen and that I should expect them. Besides, all of my life I've heard the saints say things like, "They talked about Jesus" or "They lied on Jesus" or any of a series of other statements meant to convince you that you're no better than Jesus and that any maltreatment that you're experiencing is nothing new or out of the ordinary. Furthermore, if you don't want to "buy into" the proverbial, "they say," remember the words that Jesus himself spoke in John 15:20: "The servant is not greater than his lord. If they have persecuted me, they will also persecute you," and we all know that later in his life, they did so. So, that's why you.

<u>Next, let's look at number 2</u>: Now, what do I do to get rid of my pain? How will God heal me?

We could look at quite a few passages in the scriptures in which people were hurt and had to be healed to help us to figure out what to do when we've been hurt and we're waiting for our healing, but when I think of people in the Bible who were done wrong, I immediately think of Jesus Christ. However, for our purposes, I will use Joseph because his hurt and healing occurred over the course of twenty years. It also came at the hands of friends, family members, and his leader, all of which we have touched on in the previous chapters.

Genesis 37 tells the reader about Joseph, favorite son of Jacob, who was sold into slavery. This was done by his very own brothers, that which is analogous to our church family. How deep and cutting was the knife that was twisted into his back? How much of his life's blood did he lose in the tears that he cried as he relived the betrayal, the disloyalty, the treachery? How many nights, as he sat in the bowels of the deepest, darkest dungeons did he agonize over the pain, the anguish, the heartache that his beloved father must have felt as he listened to the copious lies told by those other men who were also partakers of his father's blood? How could he ever have even a scintilla of hope of one day recovering from this pain?

Perhaps he thought that the worst days of his life were over... but his persecution did not end there; it was only beginning. It was just part one of his persecution trilogy: the family hurt. As you will read in Genesis 39, the wife of Potiphar, Joseph's master, lied upon him and, perhaps because of his blindness to his wife's treachery or his unwillingness to open his eyes to it, Joseph was put into prison. Thus ends part two: the leadership hurt. The third part of his crucifixion chronicle started in the very place where part two ended: the prison. Because of Joseph's God-given gift to understand the meanings of dreams, he was able to give Pharaoh's butler an accurate interpretation of the dream that he had while they were there in prison together. The agreement between them was that, in return for Joseph's interpreting his dream, the butler would mention Joseph to Pharaoh and get him out of his undeserved bondage. Two full years later, Joseph was still in prison. Here ends part three: the friend hurt.

You have seen Joseph's hurt by his family, by his leader, by his friend. You have experienced the pain, the persecution, the punishment. Now we can look at how he got the healing.

The healing of his "friend hurt" took place when his friend, the chief butler, finally remembered the promise that he had made to Joseph. This memory was triggered by Pharaoh's need for someone to interpret his dreams, the same thing that had helped him to take heart during his incarceration with Joseph. When he finally remembered and lived up to his word, Joseph was brought up out of his situation. He was healed of that hurt because his friend had come back to him and done his part; he had made it right.

The healing of his "leadership hurt" took place when Joseph realized that Potiphar had not put him into prison for no reason, but that God had allowed him to be imprisoned so that he would meet the person whom he needed to meet to get to where he needed to get. He had a divine appointment with the chief butler in the dungeon. Had he not been there, he probably never would have made it to the pharaoh's palace. He included this phase of his journey as part of God's divine plan, starting with his betrayal by his brothers, to save the lives of many people (see Genesis 45).

Regarding the healing of his "family hurt," it was not until more than twenty years after he was sold by his brothers for twenty pieces of silver to the Ishmeelites and taken to Egypt that he was able to forgive them and receive his healing. It makes me wonder how many of us are hurt and hold it in our hearts for years and years. We can walk around crippled and in pain, unable to be totally free because of a wound inflicted a long time ago. Well, even though Joseph overcame his "physical" bondage, he was still imprisoned by some unforgiveness buried way down deep on the inside that was a hindrance to his total deliverance. It was not until the great famine and his brothers had come back to him for food several times that he was able to forgive them.

He had played with them like rats in a cage. He had toyed with their feelings. He had allowed them to feel some of the fear that was his when he was in quandaries that he could never have expected in life as a naïve teenager. He had made false accusations against them. He had set them up just like Potiphar's wife had set him up. He had made them to feel the highest of heights in being invited to the ultimate feast in the palace of the man who was second only to Pharaoh. Conversely, he had taken them to the deepest of depths when they were forced to even consider carrying the morbid news to their father that his youngest and most favored son Benjamin had been forced to become a servant in Egypt; they knew that this news would surely kill him.

But, Joseph could take it no longer. He could no longer abide his own duplicity. His heart started to change as he saw the agony that his brothers felt as they begged for mercy for the sake of their father. Their salty tears melted the icy covering that had formed around his heart as an insulator to the pain that he had first felt two decades earlier. He surrendered his deep anger, wept aloud deep, cleansing tears, confessed his identity, forgave them, and received his healing. Furthermore, he wanted them to forgive themselves. He understood and wanted them to understand they were simply a part of God's master plan, that this whole situation was meant to be and that it was carefully crafted by God. He revealed to them the following in Genesis 45:5–8:

> *5 Now therefore be not grieved, nor angry with yourselves, that ye sold me hither: for God did send me before you to preserve life. 6 For these two years hath the famine been in the land: and yet there are five years, in the which there shall neither be earing nor harvest. 7 And God sent me before you to preserve you a posterity in the earth, and to save your lives by a great deliverance. 8 So now it was not you that sent me hither, but God: and he hath made me a father to Pharaoh, and lord of all his house, and a ruler throughout all the land of Egypt.*

After the death of his father, Joseph again reassured and comforted his brothers who came to him in abject humility begging forgiveness and offering themselves as sacrifices for their crimes against him. As further proof of his total healing, in Genesis 50:19–21 Joseph again reiterated his absolution of them:

> *19 And Joseph said unto them, Fear not: for am I in the place of God? 20 But as for you, ye thought evil against me; but God meant it unto good, to bring to pass, as it is this day, to save much people alive. 21 Now therefore fear ye not: I will nourish you, and your little ones. And he comforted them, and spake kindly unto them.*

Now who could have known that Joseph had to be unjustly attacked, accused, imprisoned and neglected in order for God's divine plan for his life and for the life of His people to work out? We could not, he could not, but we have reassurance that God is in control of it all:

4 *For since the beginning of the world men have not heard, nor perceived by the ear, neither hath the eye seen, O God, beside thee, what he hath prepared for him that waiteth for him. (Isaiah 64:4)*

To make sure that this message was not forgotten, Paul reiterated it in 1 Corinithians 2:9 when he wrote "Eye hath not seen, nor ear heard, neither have entered into the heart of man, the things which God hath prepared for them that love him."

We have to remember that God is in control of it all and that if we love God and are called according to God's purpose, everything that we go through is working together for our benefit. It is making and shaping, molding and folding us into the image of his dear son, Jesus. Even if we don't understand what it is we're going through while we're going through it, we are to give God thanks anyway while we're in it because this is what He wants us to do.

Finally, let's look at question number 3: What can I do to make sure that I don't hurt somebody else or that somebody else doesn't hurt me?

We must all remember that because the love of God is shed abroad in our hearts by the Holy Ghost, that same love must be shown one for another and one to another. I once heard somebody say that if I have something for you but don't give it to you, it's of no use. After reading about all of the trials and tribulations that all of the people whom I've written about herein experienced, we should surely all go back and reread and reapply the Golden Rule. All of the hurt and pain that has been doled out through the years under the banner of "church" could be eliminated if we would just think about how others feel.

Even other world religions and philosophies have some form of love creed; love for your fellow man and how to treat him:

Yoruba proverb (Nigeria): "One going to take a pointed stick to pinch a baby bird should first try it on himself to feel how it hurts."

Confucianism: "Do not do to others what you do not want them to do to you."

Roman Pagan Religion: "The law imprinted on the hearts of all men is to love the members of society as themselves."

53

Socrates: "Do not do to others that which would anger you if others did it to you."

Now, since this book was written from a Christian perspective, I shall end this writing with the following biblical passages which are based on the second great commandment in Matthew 22:39 where Jesus told the Pharisees that they should love their neighbor as they loved themselves. All of them, you will notice, contain the three words "love," "one," and "another":

34 *A new commandment I give unto you, That ye love one another; as I have loved you, that ye also love one another.* **35** *By this shall all men know that ye are my disciples, if ye have love one to another. (John 13:34–35)*

12 *This is my commandment, That ye love one another, as I have loved you.* **13** *Greater love hath no man than this, that a man lay down his life for his friends. (John 15:12–13)*

17 *These things I command you, that ye love one another. (John 15:17)*

10 *Be kindly affectioned one to another with brotherly love; in honour preferring one another; (Romans 12:10)*

8 *Owe no man any thing, but to love one another: for he that loveth another hath fulfilled the law. (Romans 13:8)*

13 *For, brethren, ye have been called unto liberty; only use not liberty for an occasion to the flesh, but by love serve one another. (Galatians 5:13)*

2 *With all lowliness and meekness, with longsuffering, forbearing one another in love; (Ephesians 4:2)*

9 *But as touching brotherly love ye need not that I write unto you: for ye yourselves are taught of God to love one another. (1 Thessalonians 4:9)*

24 *And let us consider one another to provoke unto love and to good works: (Hebrews 10:24)*

22 *Seeing ye have purified your souls in obeying the truth through the Spirit unto unfeigned love of the brethren, see that ye love one another with a pure heart fervently: (1 Peter 1:22)*

8 *Finally, be ye all of one mind, having compassion one of another, love as brethren, be pitiful, be courteous:*
(1 Peter 3:8)

11 *For this is the message that ye heard from the beginning, that we should love one another. (1 John 3:11)*

23 *And this is his commandment, That we should believe on the name of his Son Jesus Christ, and love one another, as he gave us commandment. (1 John 3:23)*

7 *Beloved, let us love one another: for love is of God; and every one that loveth is born of God, and knoweth God. (1 John 4:7)*

11 *Beloved, if God so loved us, we ought also to love one another. (1 John 4:11)*

12 *No man hath seen God at any time. If we love one another, God dwelleth in us, and his love is perfected in us. (1 John 4:12)*

5 *And now I beseech thee... not as though I wrote a new commandment unto thee, but that which we had from the beginning, that we love one another. (2 John 1:5)*

So it seems that the answer to this question about assuring that we don't hurt others has certainly been thoroughly addressed in the multiple scriptures cited above. Now to maybe help others not to hurt us, we could... hmm.... Let me see. We could give them a copy of this book (big smile)... in love, of course.